Workshop Material

TRUST
Partnership

Pathways to freedom

To Terry,
keep to the path,
Dave

David Crabb

TRUST Partnerships

David Crabb

First Edition 2020

© David Crabb

"Two are better than one, because they have a good return for their labour; if either of them falls down, one can help the other up. But pity anyone who falls and has no one to help them up. Also, if two lie down together, they will keep warm. But how can one keep warm alone? Though one may be over-powered, two can defend themselves. A cord of three strands is not easily broken."
Ecclesiastes 4:9-12.

Table of Contents

Foreword

When we deal with the intimate issues of life, we need to know that we can TRUST those whom we allow into that area of our lives.

David Crabb is a person you can trust implicitly. You can for two reasons: Firstly, he has been there himself. Secondly, he has a God given desire to help you. Let those words digest within you, he wants to help you and he can help you.

He is professionally qualified to do so, he most certainly has the experience, but mostly, he has a heart and a vision to do so. I thank God that He raises up people like David and his wife Sheila who give persistent time and effort in training in fields that help them to become credible, in order that they can bring hope and solutions into common areas of difficulty.

Be assured, there are lots of people struggling with the issues you may be facing. Be further assured that there are experts out there, trained by God Himself who can help you to find total freedom. Dave Crabb is such a person. I cannot do justice with mere words for an endorsement of this excellent ministry. Absorb the content of this booklet, contact the Crabb's and take their advice, join their programme and soon you will know how you can overcome and live life free from any bondage of the past.

Rev. John Bullock soulcamp.org
Introduction

"Better guide well the young than reclaim them when old,
For the voice of true wisdom is calling.
'To rescue the fallen is good, but 'tis best
To prevent other people from falling.'
Better close up the source of temptation and crime
Than deliver from dungeon or galley;
Better put a strong fence 'round the top of the cliff,
Than an ambulance down in the valley."[1]

I first heard this quote at a conference many years ago, fascinated, I looked for the source and discovered it in the form of this poem, the above being the last verse. It is well worth googling the whole poem as referenced below, it's a great read.

I began my full-time ministry in June 1987 after my theological studies came to an end at the Elim Bible College Capel. Serving as an Assistant Pastor for a few years I was eventually ordained in April 1991, and in January the same year took over as Senior Minister at our first church.

I have not always been a Christian. My background in my formative years was one of dysfunction. Up until the age of fifteen, I had suffered a level of sexual abuse. The effect of this was to cause me to become quite

---

[1] Poem – The Ambulance Down in the valley – Joseph Malins (1895)

introverted, full of shame, finding it difficult to form lasting relationships.

At the age of fifteen I decided to leave home and join the Royal Navy. I was so small and immature, 5ft 2" and weighing in at 6 stone 7llbs. It was decided that I could join, on the understanding that I still had a lot of growing left in me. It was 15th February 1971 (decimal day for those who remember).

Whilst in the Royal Navy, I realised very quickly that I would find it hard to survive were I to remain so quiet and withdrawn. I had to adopt a different kind of identity in order that I could more easily fit into the context I was now a part of.

Needless to say, my main education in regard to my sexual journey was to take place in the bars, brothels and porn palaces found in many of the countries I visited over those first few years. I became outwardly loud, brash, immature and playing a role I knew I was not. In effect I was already very conflicted in so many ways. Similar to the 'Talented Mr. Ripley' to quote him, *"I'd rather be a fake somebody than a real nobody."*[2]

For many years I carried the guilt and shame of what I got up to in the Navy, my conflicts in regard to the abuses that also took place in my younger years, all of

---

[2] 'The Talented Mr. Ripley' is a 1999 American psychological thriller directed by Anthony Minghella and starring Matt Damon.

which I was to carry into a future that was in stark contrast to such a life.

During my early years as a Christian I was not really bothered to any great degree by this past, I was revelling in my new-found identity in Christ. It was only as I took on more responsibilities and came under new stresses and pressures that the cracks began to show in my soul.

I carried much of this guilt and shame up until 2004 when during a writing trip with a great friend, John Bullock, I found a soul who really understood my journey, for he too had taken a similar path. In a hotel room in Dar Es' Salaam Tanzania, during a writing/mission's trip, amid jesting and reminiscing, John jokingly challenged me to 'fess up.'

I found myself blurting it all out, not only things from my past, but present challenges and temptations I was really struggling with. There were tears, laughter, connecting as John also opened his life to me. One of the few moments I remember where I really connected in an intimate and honest way with another male.

It was out of this context, as well as being tired of receiving the regular messages of another minister removed over moral issues, that I really began my journey toward discovering answers to the questions burning in my heart.

Why? How? I concluded very swiftly that although I now had a born-again Spirit, my soul would take a lifetime to reach maturity. I knew as a Pastor that my role was to help others reach maturity, therefore, I had to find paths myself that actually worked and were well trodden by myself and others.

This little booklet is to give a model that I have been using now to help myself and others. I'm sure it is not unique, just as I am merely another who has walked this particular road. However, my story, like anyone else's is unique and my hope and prayer is that you find some help and comfort in these few pages.

Christians believe that we are created beings and therefore we need to discover what the creator's original intention was/is for His creation. Because we are created in God's image, it seems reasonable to assert that our heavenly father simply wants to see that image restored in His children.

The passage from the book of Romans[3] makes it very clear in declaring the unveiling of the 'sons of God.' So, on that understanding, for someone to be in recovery from sexual sin, or wanting to maintain their sexual purity, presupposes that they are on a journey to recover God's original intention to truly reflect His image in His creation. I like to speak on 'original glory' not just 'original sin.'

The first step to that occurring happened at our Spiritual re-birth when we were 'born again.' A spiritual re-birth

---

[3] Romans 8:19.

was and is absolutely necessary in order for us to be 'His' children. Once we are born again, the Holy Spirit begins the work of sanctification, which is an on-going transformation – the whole process of becoming more like Jesus. Spiritual salvation is an event; sanctification is a process that continues until we are made like unto Him. God continues to bring discipline and correction, especially during seasons of sin and rebellion. God may well expose an area of our lives and encourage us to be earnest and repent.[4]

Before commencing the course, it is important for you to understand that sexual addiction is an issue in your *Soul,* that affects your body and most certainly your spiritual destiny. There are many spiritual people who carry afflictions in the Soul area of their lives, that if left unopposed, will most certainly create a disaster, or at least hamper you in terms of your spiritual destiny.

We often treat the area of sexuality differently and overlook the gross character and personality deficiencies rampant in the church today.

For many, sexuality has become a way of life. Sexual behaviours that you can turn to over and over again, with a progressive increase in the compulsions and urges, that also have a commensurate increase in the consequences. Society is soaked in a plethora of sexualised content, it is almost impossible to escape its pervasive influence, it could be described as 'predatory.'

---

[4] Revelation 3:19.

This booklet, is not a 'quick fix' to the increasing problem of sexual addictions of any kind. To be succinct, 'there are no quick fixes' to this kind of behaviour. Of course, as Christians, we hold out for a miraculous solution to all of life's issues, however, for many, more often than not, a process/journey is required. This is often the character of sanctification that leads toward transformation. Journeying alone is not recommended, especially in regard to our sexual purity.

Neither are the sessions or this booklet an attempt to describe the nature of our sexualised society, there are many materials out there that will do that. Our society is what it is, the only way we can change it, as Christians, is to challenge our own responses to it, refusing to conform to the pressures and demands that ensue from it.

Needless to say, many people attend the workshops for varying reasons. Some come merely to increase their understanding of the issues, others to obtain resources to help toward recovery, but many come, because in truth they have experienced problems in this area at some level.

Our **Mission** is to provide a 'safe space' for the exploration of the issues, as well as helping individuals who feel they are spiralling out of control, also encouraging on-going accountability groups.

Our **Values** are encapsulated in the words of Jesus.[5]

The whole concept of 'restoring to purity' is pro-active. The partnership groups that will hopefully form after the workshop concludes are not only in order to help in our discipleship and our maintaining sexual purity, but also to encourage the pro-active pursuit toward restoration. The groups are therefore not merely a reactive response to sin, they are also pro-active in pursuing the character of Christ.

The bibles exhortation is that we have everything we need for life and godliness.[6] The groups will hopefully become a place where men and women re-learn holiness, where they experience mercy triumphing over judgment. It is not our intention to minimise sin and its pervasive nature, rather, to maximise the mercy, love and ultimate power of Christ Jesus in helping us to experience the victory already won for us.[7]

A Word about Trust Partnerships

Over the years that I have been using this material, I have personally taken on men into a coaching/pastoral supervision or counselling relationship. It is a professional service for which they pay for and thereby value. However, those who do not feel they are out of control may prefer to start up TRUST partnerships. These are made up of small groups, pairs or triplet

---

[5] John 13:34-35.
[6] 2 Peter 1:3
[7] Romans 8:19-21, 1 Thessalonians 4:3-4,

groups and act as a means of accountability and support. I remain available to bring either pastoral support, supervision or personal coaching.

I would add at this point that apart from counselling training, I am a trained Life Coach and also trained in Pastoral Supervision. I have trained as a course regional trainer and was, for a period of time, a board member of the ACC (Association of Christian Counsellors). I am a Senior Member of the ACCPH (Accredited Counsellors, Coaches, Psychotherapists and Hypnotherapists) and of course still an accredited active retired Elim minister. I am now working as the Deputy Centre Manager of Willoughby House Teen Challenge UK, a drug/alcohol rehabilitation unit and Leadership Academy.

There are many books that have been written on the subject of sexuality, as well as a plethora of training materials. However, TRUST groups are about accountability and partnership, accountability is a large part of being a disciple of Jesus Christ.

The whole concept of either restoring or maintaining purity is pro-active. The pairs, triplets or groups play a huge role in encouraging one another toward restoration of purity in all areas of our lives. Good pastoral care is not merely 'reactive' but 'proactive' (seeking the lost sheep) in nature. So, holiness, purity, wholeness is a pursuit.

My prayer has always been that the groups will become for men a place where they experience mercy triumphing over judgement. It is not my intention to minimise sin or its effects in anyway, rather, to maximise the mercy of Christ. It is not enough for us to be punitive in our responses to the fallen, restoration is always gentle, bearing in mind our own frailty. Bearing in mind also the analogy of fences at the top of the cliff, not just ambulances at the bottom.

If the Church focuses on God judging and punishing, then the Church should expect those things to begin among them first! King David in the classic Psalm 51 called on God for mercy concerning his own sin. He begged that the Lord would not take away the Holy Spirit from his life. He also promised to teach other transgressors the ways of the Lord and help them turn back to God.

You can only revive what is dying. This is why Jesus Himself said that, 'only the sick need the doctor.'[8] The same applies to the call for the restoration of purity – we do so out of the understanding that worldliness, impurity, compromise and mediocrity have crept into our own lives. My workshop is centred on restoring and maintaining sexual purity in our lives.
There are three main headings we can use in defining someone who is trapped in sexual sin. These three headings in some way also clarify the varying levels of sinful behaviour, which if left unchecked, will almost certainly result in living at a level not meant for the believer.

---

[8] Mark 2:17

It must be understood right from the outset that fundamentally we are 'born again, children of God,' that in our Spirits we are perfect. However, we also acknowledge that in respect to our Souls, we are damaged goods, in recovery and learning how to remain free. It is also a fact that recovery will never be achieved alone or in isolation. Isolation is the very last thing anyone truly in recovery needs. It is difficult to talk of these matters, in particular the sexual aspect of our lives, however, it is necessary for us to be in the light with one another.

Three areas of definition:

- o Sexual Lust
- o Sexual Acting Out
- o Sexual Addiction

Lust – defined as a strong sexual impulse. Within the context of our study, lust is a burning for what is not rightfully ours.

Acting Out – The physical expression of internal lust.

Addiction – Where lusting and acting out have become unmanageable.

It appears there are three main ways in which we deal with Christians who fall into an area of sexual sin (this is not an exhaustive list, merely the main points). The first way is to **remove them from fellowship**. A church membership reacts in utter shock and the righteous remove the offender from the congregation and make it extremely difficult for them to return.

The reason this occurs in in order for a rapid solution to be found and in order that life within the church is not seen as hypocritical and can return to normal as soon as possible. However, this leaves no room for Grace and Mercy toward the sinner who may well be repentant; it also leaves no room for the possible restoration of the offender and little room for the pastoral care of those more fully impacted by their actions.

To remove without any recourse to restoration, denies the bibles mandate to bring a person back into fellowship through a process of restoration and discipline, along with the undergirding principles of grace and mercy. In fact, this process should be a major distinctive in the church of Jesus Christ.

A second way is to **ignore it altogether** in the hope that it will just stop. This is called denial and is sin upon sin. Where people all know about the sin but choose to simply ignore it and not confront anyone. Some people use the passage in Matthew 7:1-5 in justifying this kind of behaviour. They suggest that Jesus is saying that we should not judge one another, but we need to understand that what Jesus is confronting here is the hypocritical judgement of one another, in pretending to be absolutely holy and pure ourselves.

It is with humility and in the fear of God that we deal with one another. In doing so we encourage righteous and holy living as opposed to going on witch hunts in order to merely expose people.

Finally, there can be the 'forgive and forget' kind of attitude that could be more readily described as 'cheap grace.' In other words, providing the sinner is sorry we should forgive immediately, encourage everyone to simply forget about it and move on, returning the sinner to positions they once held almost immediately.

Those taking this course are proud of their merciful and gracious attitudes and consider themselves as ultra-spiritual. They neglect to note that in fact restoration also involves the confrontation or demolition of wrong character traits and the rebuilding of correct ones. This will involve pro-active pastoring/coaching.

The quick fix method is a popular one because deep down it is how we want to be dealt with ourselves, but it dismisses too readily and easily the deeper issues associated with someone caught in sin and the need for radical process. Forgive and forget actually robs someone of the God given opportunity for a true, deep and lasting repentance and almost encourages a relapse in the future.

True restoration comes through a process of measured discipline, soaked in mercy and guided through responsibility, aiming to help someone back to a God centred life. This can be a challenge to pastoral leadership that focuses mainly on leadership/preaching, there needs to be the release of the 'pastors' to care for the flock they have charge for.

If a church chooses the path of denial and opts for a much quicker resolution, restoration is consequently provided almost instantly. Instant restoration to a position that has ignored the need for 'truth' and full disclosure regarding the sin, along with complete repentance and fruit and the re-establishing of spiritual identity and discipline will always fail.

A **motivation** exercise. Write down as many reasons you can think of for wanting to reclaim or maintain your sexual purity, review these motives regularly.

Accountability. The recognition and acceptance that your sexual purity will not be regained and maintained if you remain in isolation. The willingness to be open and honest about where you are personally is paramount. The need to allow others to input you and for you to be regular in your attendance to the group and available to other members of the group is equally important.

Pilgrimage – In the Christian classic pilgrim's progress by John Bunyan, the character Christian realises that he has a burden that is distracting him, it is draining him and ultimately destroying him. When asked by his mentor why he is just *standing there,'* with this burden, his answer pictures what many men would probably say today, *"I don't know where to turn?"* You can read all the books and listen to the famous preachers, but this issue cannot be dealt with through information alone, you cannot remain isolated.

Most people know when they have a problem, but guilt and shame, even confusion keeps them anchored to the issue and seemingly spiritually emasculated. Recovery only really begins when someone dares to step out of the shadows of isolation and engages with others on the same journey. One of the reasons many twelve step programmes can be so effective.

Sexual sin begins in distracting a person, eventually it will begin to drain them, as they have to live in a world of cover up; lies; fear of exposure and the like. Destruction in all kinds of areas can be the result. Real relationships are therefore uncommon as their ability to experience genuine intimacy is directly affected.

I have started the 'TRUST partnership' as a means of bridging this gap. Either become part of, or start up a group you are comfortable in. If you feel you are out of control you can contact me via my website for help. Don't remain alone – you don't have to.

Chapter One – Turning Around

For anyone to progress from seeing themselves as simply 'damaged goods,' will involve being willing to completely give up the behaviour that we know is inappropriate at least, and downright wrong at worst.

It does not take too long for wrong behaviour to become part of what would be considered as normal routine for us. It comes naturally to us to imbibe practices and habits very quickly. Our brains develop neural pathways easily and it takes repetition to correct these kinds of things.[9]

Sexual sin offers a significant, intensely pleasurable experience (otherwise we would not become so easily entangled). Much like a drug addict, who experiences a 'big hit' and expends his life chasing after that hit again. Each subsequent experience requires more and more hyper stimulation.

An illegitimate sexual experience will hyper-stimulate and eventually require a more intense experience as time goes on. It is very easy for someone to become comfortable with this kind of behaviour and even convince themselves it is relatively harmless and controllable – IT IS NOT!

---

[9] See 2 Corinthians 10:3-5.

No matter how intense the experience, no matter how seemingly harmless, eventually it will lead to destruction. That can occur in a marriage, a job, a ministry; we stand to lose so much.

What is genuinely meaningful becomes secondary to the addiction, our relationship with God, our family, our self- respect, all seem to lose their significance in our lives, we fail to see how close to complete meltdown we are. That is when God intervenes.

What kind of patterns might cause God to intervene in a person's life? Well the answer to that question is broken down into three areas mentioned earlier in the introduction.

1. Sexual Lust. Described as an illegitimate burning for what is not rightfully ours. Unfortunately, 'lust' is a trait that our own culture has become comfortable with and therefore it is so much easier for the Christian to become comfortable with it also. However, Jesus described it as very serious when He declared it to be as serious as actual physical adultery. James said it is the beginning of the end.[10]

2. Acting Out. If lust is not apprehended Immediately it will lead to the pressure to 'act out.' This may take us way beyond the boundaries of created intent and may include: Pornography use; habitual

---

[10] Matthew 5:28, James 1:15.

masturbation; various forms of fornication; adultery; strip clubs; prostitutes and the like. It is important to note that young men experience an incredible hormonal rush during their teens, resulting in spontaneous erections, wet dreams and the like. Great care, common sense and understanding is needed at this time of life, as a younger person's maturation progresses.

3.   The final straw is '**Sexual addiction,**' the patterns of lusting and acting out become totally unmanageable. Addiction is when the acting out becomes a normal part of our routine and we have learned to live with it. However, like any addiction, there are incredible consequences.[11]

Am I addicted?

Think about what it is that drew you either to the workshop, the course or an accountability group. Acceptance that you have a problem is a major step. Have you started a journey because you realise you cannot deal with this alone? Or has someone suggested or even insisted you do something? See the additional scripture below.[12]

"In order for God to bring a person to the place of recovery, they are required to face up to their behaviour, so God brings this behaviour to their attention."

---

[11] Phil 2:3, Psalm 138:8, Phil 1:6, 1 Tim 2:4, John 3:3, 1 Thessalonians 4:3-4, Revelation 3:19, Matthew 5:28, James 1:5.
[12] Proverbs 5:22, 2 Peter 2:19.

The word that the Bible uses for addiction is 'bondage.' Whenever we engage in using porn for instance, it is as though we are literally binding ourselves up in the very cords of that behaviour. Sexual freedoms promulgated during the 'so called' sexual revolution undergird and endorse the very things that bind so many.

It is the behaviour that becomes addictive more so than the sex itself. This is because the behaviour is 'hyper stimulating' things such as pornography or anonymous encounters etc. The fantasy promises so much, but the reality can be sordid, sickening even.

The acting out begins to increase in frequency; it continues to increase in intensity. Impotence can result in some men, because the human system becomes accustomed to, and adjusts itself to the hyper stimulation; the consequence of this is sometimes a person finds it difficult to engage in what was once their normal sexual experience.

Addiction is revealed through a person's seeming inability to stop their behaviour, they may have seasons where they may stop for a short time, but something occurs to trigger the recommencement of the behaviour. If this is the case it is time to recognise there is a very real problem. However, many do not.

Things may continue until the addiction begins to intrude upon our everyday lives. Family, finances, even the physical, professional or legal areas.

Family. Your family deserves and indeed needs your time, energy and focussed attention. Bondage or addiction is distracting and will intrude into your family life, this means you may be redirecting time and attention elsewhere and thereby cheating on them.

Finances. It may begin by simply using some of the extra cash available but can easily lead to using the money for the mortgage, or holiday money, school savings for the children??

Physical/Professional/Legal. It is possible, even likely, that many forms of acting out involve physical risks and exposure to STD's or harmful acts. You could be taking professional risks that lead to job loss or exposure at work.

The worst thing with any addiction is the ever-increasing demand for greater forms of stimulation, which may even lead to acting out in an illegal way. Downloading questionable pornography, under age prostitutes, trafficked prostitutes, public indecency. These areas reveal that a person is doing things that are not only out of character, but foolish, which in itself reveals that bondage leads to the interruption of volitional ability. Here are some questions worth asking at this point:

1. How can I practically (and radically) separate myself from this kind of behaviour?
2. What will my life be like in five years if I continue in this way?
3. What would you envision your life to be like if you can cease this behaviour?

The beginning of the end!! *"God begins the process of 'Turning Around" into a person's life by sending a crisis of truth. It begins in 'knowing the truth' before the truth can set you free."*

The trouble all began with a lie. When Eve was lied to in the Garden of Eden, the lie had three primary ingredients to it, all of which are repeated − even today.

- o God doesn't really understand you, or your needs. (A lie about God).
- o The thing you're tempted by will not destroy you. (A lie about self).
- o It will be life enhancing, make you happy. (A lie about life).

God may well begin the crisis of truth Internally, that is, through our conscience which may well still be fairly sensitive to the Holy Spirit. You may flatter yourself in knowing all the scriptures, however, are they real to you? Are they working in your life? This internal crisis may continue for quite some time as God gives us time to repent. However, this should not be interpreted as permission to continue in the behaviour, this is because we are primarily consequence driven.

God does not delight in allowing us to be exposed, but as someone once said, *"If you try to be in public what you are not being in private, God may allow your private to become public."*[13]

---

[13] Dr. Edwin Louis Cole, author of Maximised manhood, founder of Christian men's network.

The crisis will eventually come externally. This might be through a level of exposure or, in some cases, even tragedy. For instance, the exposure may come through the word of God which a person then chooses to ignore. They also ignore their conscience meaning God then speaks through circumstances which cannot be ignored.

The crisis hopefully will generate enough fear of God or anger over perceived loss to move a person into action. Action is what 'Turning Around' is all about. It is literally STOP what you are doing and turn around.

It is more than confession which is acknowledgement of wrong; it is more than a stated intent, it is literally actions we take, radical steps to ensure we do not do it again. That we interrupt in a radical way the strongholds that have been formed in our souls. To turn around and go in another direction is total separation, getting radical, doing whatever is necessary.

Jesus spoke radically about plucking out eyes, severing limbs to illustrate this.[14] We then turn toward that which we know is right. Repentance is always connected to faith.

---

[14] Matthew 5:29.

Chapter Two - Rules that Restore – Re-ordering our lives- bringing structure

At this juncture I want to encourage you to begin to keep a journal. It is healthy and helpful to write down your thoughts each day and can be very enlightening and indeed encouraging to review your progress as you continue in new or renewed disciplines.

A quick reminder.

Author Jim Collins wrote two very significant books that outline the absolute need for us to 'know' **how** we are, and how that question cannot be answered alone.[15]

Collins was asked the question from a chief executive of one of America's most successful companies, *"We've had tremendous success in recent years, and I worry about that. I want to know; how do you know? When you are at the top of the world, the most powerful nation on earth, the most successful company in your industry, the best player in your game, your very power and success might cover up the fact that you're already on the path to decline. So, how would you know?"*

This arises from Collins assertion that a country has a responsibility to renew itself constantly, history teaches us this. All the old empires that have existed failed to renew themselves and consequently went into decline. The

---

[15] Good to Great & How the Mighty Fall.

same can happen with individuals. But how do we know we are in danger of decline if we are successful on the surface of things? This has been my cry to Church leaders for a number of years now. It is tempting for a leader to judge and value him or herself based on an 'external locus.' In other words, if the performance is going well, they assume they are well.

Decline can be analogous to disease, perhaps like a cancer, that can grow on the inside while on the outside everything still looks healthy and strong.

Collins identifies five stages

1. **Stage 1** - Hubris born of success – where success can give a forward momentum that can continue even when leaders make poor decisions or choices or fail to look after themselves. (We're so great we can do anything).

2. **Stage 2 -** An undisciplined pursuit of more, straying from a disciplined growth, in the case of an individual this could be likened to someone getting too much too soon without the emotional, intellectual and psychological capacity to contain it.

3. **Stage 3** – Denial of risk and peril – warning signs begin to show but external success allows them to be explained away, giving a false sense of

security. Those in power blame external circumstances for any kind of failure, dialogue disappears and high- risk decisions are made.

4. **Stage 4** – Grasping for salvation – the bad decisions begin to show and control, a decline begins that is visible to all, quick fixes are sought out, quick and easy solutions to bring back to earlier success. Sometimes a charismatic solution is looked for, a saviour, a visionary.

5. **Stage 5** – Capitulation to irrelevance or death – the longer we remain in stage 4 the   more likely degeneration will continue. Eventually there is an abandonment of any great future there is atrophy into utter insignificance.

Although this is written with companies in mind the metaphors are easily applicable to the individual. Leaving the question, *"how do you know?"* A very relevant question, that needs to be considered. A reminder, please do not try to do this alone, get help, get connected.

Pastoral reflective practice, also known as supervision, is a means for someone to be able to ask that question, How do you know? Coaching, mentoring any of these skills require the interaction of two or more people.

Pride can be the factor that stops us (particularly leaders) from instigating a 'pastoral supervision/reflective practice' or indeed a 'coaching' relationship in our lives.

We will look at some of the more obvious disciplines such as devotions; recommitments; bible reading; prayer; fellowship in accountability; establishing of close friendships. The word rules can often be offensive to Christians because the argument would be that we are called to live by grace, however, establishing rules in our lives demonstrates a determination to regain order.

When a person is struggling in addictive behavior, more often than not one of the tell-tale signs is a lack of order and discipline in their lives. Discipline will involve us setting ourselves boundaries where there were none, or where they have been crossed. In fact, Christians should not be offended with this as to be a disciple is to be a 'disciplined one.'

It is one thing to have the desire to be back on track in our relationship with God and with others, it is quite another thing to be back on track in our relationship with God and with others, it is quite another thing to be able to maintain that initial zeal. It is through building structure into our lives and reestablishing disciplines that we are more likely to remain in a place of recovery. This most certainly means having some form of accountability, to help us in forming these areas consistently.

1. **Daily Devotions**. This is often one of the most neglected areas of discipline in the lives of many Christians. A focused and consistent time where we are separated to God, spending time reading the scriptures; praying; perhaps also reading devotional material to help inspire and teach us. It is vital we aim for consistency, not just volume. Rushing in and having a two-hour devotional time seems impressive IF you are having it consistently-daily. It would be more useful to have 30 minutes if it becomes part of your normal, daily, structure.

2. **Your Bible**. Is the most important tool you have during this time. Books are ok, but it is the constant soaking in God's word that will bring the most help. A useful way of reading the Bible is to spend time in each section ie New Testament, Old Testament and perhaps the Psalms and Proverbs. There are some excellent reading plans available.

Learning to pray is vital as that is how our intimacy with God is developed. Journaling is a habit I began in 1984, it helps to track what has been and is going on in our lives and our intimate times with God. Sometimes I like to write out my prayers, writing down my intimate thoughts helps order them and understand what it is I am wanting to communicate. The most important thing is that everything is kept simple and consistent, that we learn to value the time and enjoy it, looking forward to escaping with God.

Something else that is useful in this time is to review our motivations, what is it that we are really aiming for on the personal level? If, for example, it is to maintain sexual purity, then it is good to daily remind yourself of that fact. Perhaps even an 'out loud' statement of intent, calling on God for strength for the day.

Our daily devotion is a discipline that we are maintaining ourselves, that is, the only other person involved is God. However, it is also important that we seek to develop relationships or alliances with others. These are relationships that we bring into our lives in order to make ourselves more accountable and transparent, especially during a recovery time.

Our biggest enemy to forming these alliances will always be 'time.' It takes time to meet and schedule future meetings. It will also require humility, a willingness to be vulnerable; maybe even a degree of inconvenience. The simple fact of the matter is, if we were able to accomplish sexual recovery or maintenance ourselves we would have achieved it by now.[16]

If in recovery!

When in recovery, especially during the early days, there are various types of alliances we may need to form – some of them on a more formal level.

Mentors: Perhaps a pastor or maybe even a counsellor.[17] These will be meetings that will require setting up meetings in advance. I recommend at least monthly meetings in my own practice, especially in recovery situations, as longer than that invites a likelihood of relapse.

I mention possibly having a counsellor as they are trained to help, especially where there are considerations such as depression, or indeed psychotherapeutic areas to journey through. Do not baulk at the idea of 'paying' for these services. Your pastor is paid, usually via the offerings collected in church, counsellors are professional people who have invested a lot into training, continual professional development, their own supervision and membership of ethical bodies. Many counsellors will take into consideration a person's 'means' in their decisions on fees.

Simply put, your recovery has to be worth investing into.

Depending upon the severity of the issue, there may be a need to visit a G.P. most certainly where severe

---

[16] Proverbs 13:20.
[17] Proverbs 20:18.

depression is a factor. It may be that a counsellor will recommend you visit a G.P. It can be that sexual addiction in particular affects every area of our life, there may even be other associations or cross addictions to consider.

A peer relationship is very useful, someone you perhaps go to the gym with, or some other kind of pursuit. Peer relationships are vital, especially when you just need a friend alongside you, someone to encourage you.

If we refuse accountability we tend to harden our hearts when left alone. When we are accountable to others it almost acts like a mirror, reflecting back to us our strengths, weaknesses, dreams and visions. Any accountability is not punitive, but for exhorting, teaching, encouraging, and at times confronting behaviour. Men often find it difficult to know where to look for accountability.

Options:
An experienced pastoral practitioner/spiritual director.

A counsellor – who will watch over your mental and emotional health.

G.P. The trauma of exposure or other factors such as anxiety, depression, loss of esteem, insomnia etc.

Existing men's or women's groups.

Accountability groups (such as TRUST partnerships).

Existing friendships/family.

Financial advisor, where there have been financial consequences to behaviour.

Essentially you need people in your life with the maturity to commit to regular meetings, to ask what are the difficult questions, someone who shares your vision to grow. Someone who knows of your blind spots and are unafraid to confront when they sense either denial or a refusal to face up to areas in our lives. The closest accountability partner will need to know certain things, so you need to be sure of their own personal integrity. What has been/is your acting out behaviour? What are your general goals? What is your progress? Helping you to form strategies.

Something that is often overlooked when dealing with the whole process of recovery and maintenance is the need for social and play time. This whole process can be very tiring, draining and intense and we need to include some social and play time into our routine.[18]

The final consideration in the re-structuring of our lives and one of the most challenging areas is appreciating the effects of sexual sin on those around us.

There is no easy way to say this. Sexual sin is a betrayal of trust and therefore will, without doubt, have an effect

---

[18] Proverbs 17:22.

on those who are close enough to have trusted us. When a person truly repents of their sexual acting out, they will not only be focussed on making sure it does not happen again, they will also begin to show concern for those closest to them.

Our sin affects others – God; our spouse; family members; church; close friends. To make restitution therefore is to seek to restore what we've wrongly taken or caused to be lost. For instance, in the case of a married man it is almost certain that your wife's assumptions about you have died, or at the least, put her in a place of severe trial concerning her trust in you.

How can a wife's confidence in you have been affected?

- They can lose confidence in themselves in various ways – for e.g. their attractiveness.
- Their intelligence – for failing to see any signs that now seem so obvious.
- Their significance can be affected – 'I was not enough!'
- Confidence in God can be affected – (Why didn't God show me?).
- Comfort they derived from being in what they thought was a safe relationship (who can I truly trust now).

Forgiveness may come easier than the restoration of confidence and trust – this will most certainly take time. For those in recovery the hardest part can be in the total acknowledgment of the nature of what has been done, the consequences caused, the understanding of the pain brought into the lives of those we love.

An expression of remorse is only a starting point and must not degenerate into tearful, perpetual self-pity. Our loved ones will need to be assured of the intentions and plan of action and the form our recovery will take. Those involved in the recovery process will need to be tough during this part, for the temptation will be to try and minimise the acknowledgment and the need to express genuine remorse.

Understandably, the person in recovery will want to get this part over with as soon as possible; however, those who become victimised to an extent through the consequences arising from this behaviour will almost certainly require time. They deserve time, especially if they have indicated that they are willing for the relationship to be saved.

What acknowledgment can look like.

- I know and accept that what I did has devastated you and that you have understandably lost confidence in me.
- I know that this is a betrayal of your trust in me.
- I know that I have broken my commitment to you.
- I know that it is up to me to seek to rebuild that trust, that it will not happen overnight.
- I know that I have damaged our relationship.

- I do not fully understand the pain I have caused you.
- I do not really know how you feel.
- Help me to understand how you feel, I agree to always try hard to listen.

Express:

- My actions prove that I am the one in the wrong and I am in pain over what I have done to you and our relationship.
- I hope you will, in time, forgive me.
- My words alone cannot hope to change things, please watch my actions.
- Can I share my plan of action with you?

I know, I know this all seems really heavy. Some may resent this kind of approach, citing the famous preachers who admit adultery one week and are back in the pulpit the following. I have no comment to make on that, except that accountability is for our own sake as much as those around us.

Recovery is not just about the one in recovery, it is about recovering the 'true self' and all that has been lost whilst the 'false self' ran rampage. To convince another that we are committed to real change will take much more than just words. After all, it was your word to your loved one that now lays in tatters as it were. Seeking therefore to bring restitution will hopefully, eventually, restore a degree of trust and confidence in your word again. In time, things could even be stronger than before, for now the 'true self' is fully restored.

Now the need and value for accountability can be truly seen, for those in recovery will need to be disciplined as well as encouraged and sympathised with as the process becomes even more difficult.

Some practical tasks to consider.

- Block any TV channels that are not appropriate, ensure only a trusted person has the PIN number.
- Install accountability software on all computers/devices, preferably someone who is up to date on IT and knows all the loop holes. This may even require having a mobile phone that does not access the internet.
- Get rid of inappropriate movies, anything that could act as an external trigger toward acting out.
- Be honest about the kinds of environments that you know you are vulnerable in. Make a list of external triggers you are aware of and discuss them with your partner. Discuss with your counsellor or pastor the internal triggers, keep an honest account of 'how' you really are.

The environment we choose to operate within must reflect our goals and beliefs, if it does not we need to do something about it. A time for total honesty.[19]

---

[19] Colossians 3.

A brief word about stress and depression. The cause of stress can be anything that seems to make you tense, angry, frustrated or unhappy. Of course, it also has to be noted that some forms of stress can create a sense of excitement. One person's stress may be another person's excitement, some levels of stress are good for us and help us to overcome challenges and obstacles, even stopping us getting bored. Too much stress, however, affects our health and well-being, and may interfere with our jobs and social/family lives.

We all have low moods from time to time, especially according to life's circumstances or the like. This is not what is meant by depression. Depression is a far more serious illness which a person may have had for an extended period, affecting the body as well as the mind. It can come on for no reason at all, and may sometimes even be life threatening. No one symptom alone indicates whether you must have a low mood or what is termed as 'clinical depression.' Many of the symptoms can be similar, however, when you are depressed they are usually more intense and go on for longer. A simple rule of thumb is that if your low mood affects all parts of your life, lasts for two weeks or longer, even bringing you to the point of thinking about suicide, you should seek help. Depression can be treated, and you can feel better in time.

There are some very good resources to find out more about stress and depression and the effects they can have upon you. The British Medical Association provide some excellent resources to read up on.[20]

Whatever the case is, if you think you are depressed, get some medical advice in the first instance, it is better not to try and self-diagnose.

---

[20] www.bma.org.uk

Chapter Three - Understanding – gaining insight into our personal situation

Up to now we have been focussing on obedience, accountability and actions we need to take toward recovery. It is also useful and even necessary that we seek to gain insight into how or why we got to the point we did, although insight does not solve our problems, it does help us address them and manage them.[21]

I have made mention already about 'triggers' that can initiate behaviour and they usually fall into two main categories, external triggers and internal triggers. By trigger I mean something that turns you on sexually and may encourage you to pursue a course that is illegitimate and will only lead you to further actions that may result in sexual acting out.

An **external** trigger could be as simple as an erotic dream; a smell; a thought; an attractive woman or watching something inappropriate. Some of these things can actually be unavoidable especially in the cultural environment we now live in. A fleeting glance of a magazine cover? An advertising board?[22]

Sexual idolatry is actually considered normal now within our culture. It is difficult, in fact, almost impossible to avoid some things, therefore we need further understanding concerning ourselves and how we can

---

[21] 1 Thessalonians 4:3-4.
[22] 1 John 2:16, Ephesians 2:2.

cope with this kind of pressure. The first obvious thing to do practically is to reduce them as much as possible by dealing with the ones we can do something about. At the end of the previous chapter are suggestions for the obvious things that are within our control. The areas of our authority such as the home and the work place are areas that may need special attention.

It is impossible to rid our world of external triggers entirely; they are constantly in our face, they have to be accepted, but they do not have to be indulged. So, we must not take on a fatalistic attitude where we stop even trying to deal with them. Temptation is a matter of fact, especially for the Christian and it is about taking appropriate action and as the bible says, taking captive our thoughts.

The bible makes it clear that temptation is a guarantee but that the man who endures is blessed.[23] So, we should not expect a cessation of temptation, rather, we seek a different response to it. The presence of sin is constant, but the power that sin has is another matter.[24]
Removing and Responding are two key words here. Remove as many external triggers as possible and learn to respond differently to the ones that are constantly there to seek to trip us up.

Internal triggers are not always sexual in character. These kinds of triggers are not environmental, rather,

---

[23] James 1:12.
[24] 1 John 1:8, Romans 6:14.

they are initiated from within us and we will term them as wounds. A wound which causes a degree of discomfort may cause someone to seek sexual release as a way of 'medicating' the wound rather than properly deal with it. Disappointments and tragedies; are examples of wounds that can cause someone to seek to anesthetise their pain with sexual excitement. Seeking the pleasure of sexual sin is not just because a man is looking for sex, full stop, it can also be because of the afore mentioned 'hyper stimulation' that sex offers, which can be likened to a narcotic or cathartic type of effect.

Many alcoholics do not drink because they enjoy the taste, or indeed desire the social aspect, for many it is simply because it acts as an anaesthetic for a short time, until the next drink. Significant emotional wounds can still cause pain many years later, the same as unresolved issues and the like.

Men are archetypically good at hiding their wounds and often bury them or see it as weakness to talk about them or get help. Many times, I have heard counselling described as 'pink and fluffy.' In fact, my experience of going to counselling has been some of the most painful yet maturing processes I have ever experienced. Facing up to inner issues is the hardest of things to do. Another point to make here, is that there are many ways in which someone either fails to deal with a wound, or even use that wound to gain sympathy, attention, or to justify aberrant behaviour.

- Wallowing – some get into a habit of having a good old suffer, that causes them to enter a cycle of behaviour that is described as the sin/repent cycle, that impedes any progress and keeps a person operating in that cycle sometimes for years.
- Some habitually manifest the convenient usage of their wound for sympathy, relief, even attention, with no intention of moving on from it.
- Some minimise their wounds, to the extent that they see no need to address them, in fact even taking a cynical and hard-hearted view of those who do address their wounds and talk about them.
- Some discover that they have inner hurts, that have never really been dealt with – they abandon their coping mechanism, which may have been sexualised behaviour, to discover the old wound re-emerges stronger than ever.

If a person has been medicating with sexual sin, then when the sin is repented from and abandoned, the pain can become even more visible. The benefit of sexual sin is it does relieve the pain; the problem is, it can prevent us from dealing with the deeper inner issues as well as creating all kinds of new reasons for pain.

A recommended read for men is a book by John Eldridge entitled, 'Wild at Heart.' In it he identifies a wound that many men carry which he calls a wound of incompetence. The question in the hearts of many men is, 'Am I man enough? Do I have what it takes? Am I really a man?' This wound is caused by the lack of fathering. He calls it a 'father wound.' It can also arise as a result of what is termed a 'Gender role wound.' That can be caused by the expectation a culture has upon those whose role is male, confidence is in the belief (or lack of belief) in your own ability to fulfil that role. Of course, the same can be true for women who live with a cultural expectation of what it is to be a real woman.

In my own earlier life, as a young impressionable, immature teen, Gender role modelling impacted my life dramatically. It resulted in abuses of all kinds, eventually creating all kinds of wounds that still have to be faced up to today. By sinning sexually (as I did as a sailor), you attempt to create a belief in your own manhood (as modelled by your immediate culture), that is not understood at the time as dysfunctional or inappropriate. This became much more apparent to me when I entered a totally different culture as a Christian.

Feelings of insignificance can also convey a mis-belief that, 'I don't count.' It eats away at a primary need, that being to bring an impact to our environment. Humiliation is yet another wound that induces all kinds of fears.

- Fear of being looked down upon.
- Fear of being ridiculed – for e.g. men who have been humiliated in younger years.
- When a man gives himself to a woman sexually or emotionally, he gives his most sensitive parts of himself. This can result in great comfort and

strength or indeed if mishandled can cause great harm. The same applies for a woman of course.

- Humiliation of any kind will cause someone to withdraw from intimacy and create a craving to turn to things that do not require any significant investment of ourselves – such as pornography.

Action stations!![25] It is time to talk. Externalising is the first step to dealing with Internal issues. As well as the mentors mentioned previously and of course your partner, my vision is for the partnership groups or pairs or triplets will play a role in helping people experience real sharing, within a new kind of culture. There may be times of grieving that we need to be sensitive to, especially when someone is really impacted at the level of consequence their behaviour has created. This will kick start a process of healing.

Talking about sinful behaviour forces it into the light, as well as discussing how your wounds affect you and the ways in which you relate to the outside world. If you have previously withdrawn from true intimacy, this will require a concerted effort, especially when things become difficult. It will involve giving your partners permission to check on you, to ask the difficult questions.[26]

Cycles of Temptation: To pursue a lifestyle that no longer allows illegitimate sexual behaviour actually instigates adversity, one of the facts that living in a fallen

---

[25] 1 Peter 1:13.
[26] 2 Samuel 6:20.

world creates. In fact, adversity began the moment you became a Christian. Temptation does seem to come in cycles; many I have counselled or helped through pastoral supervision, speak of periods of victory which sometimes after weeks, months even years suddenly dissipate into a period of revisiting sinful behaviour (known as relapse).

This causes incredible discouragement and can lead to a total capitulation if not handled sensitively and stopped before it becomes unmanageable. In a conference a number of years ago I recall the speaker 'Sy Rogers' saying, 'God would rather have you dirty than not at all.' I wonder if we are able to take on that view? However, just because it is possible for a relapse to occur does not presuppose that it is inevitable – IT IS NOT! A lasting victory is possible and even probable, if we approach this as an accountable, disciplined person.

Sometimes it is possible to arrive at a place of paralysis and a belief that it is impossible to break free, in the Christian world this is known as 'being in bondage.' Satan is very real and the satanic world will seek to instigate a relapse in a believer, designed to act like cords that bind us up and cause us to believe it is impossible to break free. The bible makes it very clear that the arena of attack is the mind.[27]

The first time you ever sinned sexually, your brain recorded this event for future reference, including the

---

[27] 1 Peter 1:13.

heightened feelings of sexual release. Just like eating chocolate, a pleasurable experience whilst ignoring the effects of over-indulgence, such as diabetes, weight issues and the like. So, when a certain mood or trigger – external or internal, takes place, the brain tends to bring up solutions for relief. For some it may be to turn to pornography and masturbate, which enforces the neural pathways in the brain, Christians call these pathways 'strongholds.' This activity will not cease, it is the main way in which our spiritual enemy has in causing us to become ineffective and powerless in our faith. Temptation is about enticement which at that point is not sin, Jesus was tempted, we are all tempted. So, when sexual temptation arrives and we are enticed and yield, using pornography and masturbating you are no longer struggling with sin, you are 'using,' just like a drug addict.

'Stimulation leads to Entertainment leading to Indulgence.'

Stimulation describes the very first arousal. It may come as the first look or thought; you have to decide right at that point. The earlier the right choice is made, the better. A pop up comes onto your computer screen, or you have clicked on something that resulted in something you didn't expect, dallying or playing with the thought means you are in danger already. The bible recommends taking that thought captive immediately and making it obedient to Christ.[28]

---

[28] 2 Corinthians 10:3-5.

The next stage to temptation is 'entertaining,' which by this point we are already flirting with the idea of sin, it is as though we have invited the thought in to flirt a little longer with this stimulating idea. We deceive ourselves when we try to tell ourselves we will stop in a moment, action has to be immediate or we have already lost.

King David entertained the idea of sleeping with Bathsheba as he observed her bathing. The visual stimulation led to entertaining the idea of sexual activity with her, which led to it actually taking place. Which led to the final stage of **Indulgence.** It does not take very long to travel from, 'I want,' to 'I have to have.' Total relapse occurs and along with it will come the inevitable 'consequences.' Guilt, Shame, Paralysis, Bondage, Fear of exposure, Lies, Cover-up, the belief that freedom is impossible.

Deception – self-deception is an awful thing. Many years ago, on speaking with a client on one occasion, who was relating a sexual incident he had with a woman he was visiting to have a 'bible study' with. He told me, *'things just happened, I went to study with her, the next thing was, we were having sex, I didn't mean for it to happen.'* On further questioning it 'happened' that he had 'safe sex' because he 'happened' to take a condom with him for bible study?? Self-deception is characteristic with most illegitimate sexual behaviour.

TRUST Partnerships

Chapter Four - Strategy – making plans and devising strategies to succeed

At this point, it is hoped that you are well on the way to having formed a new structure of daily devotions, accountability and any other forms of help required such as mentoring/coaching/counselling or pastoral supervision. Strategy will include the following elements:

- Developing a lifestyle of confronting sin and conforming to the Holy Spirit.
- Learning to co-operate with the Holy Spirit.
- Understanding our responsibilities to invest and what we can then expect from God.
- Learning patience.
- Learning a new language.

We need to develop a strategy, being pro-active, to deal with the attacks that we know will come upon anyone at any level of recovery, or seeking to maintain sexual purity.[29] It will mean learning to confront previous mindsets (which in itself can be tiring). Confronting sin and conforming or yielding our minds and bodies to God is a continuing act of worship.

This will require cooperation between you and the Holy Spirit, by trusting God to do what we cannot do means that we are trusted by God to do what we can do. We cannot purify our own hearts and we cannot make ourselves hate sin, neither can we make someone else

---

[29] Romans 6:19.

forgive us, but these are things that God can do. What we can do is maintain our disciplines, especially our daily devotion, we can apply ourselves in confronting sin, and God will continue the transforming work within us. God will require us to invest in our strategy and time and energy are the main ways in doing this.

Developing and implementing a strategy will require patience from us and our loved ones or our accountability partners, who are involved in our recovery or maintenance with us. One of the quickest ways to abort our recovery is when we become impatient over our progress. This is why we cannot hope to do this alone. So often I come across people who declare, *'I went to two counselling sessions, took the anti-depressants, nothing has changed.'* In my experience, to build a relationship with a trusted counsellor will take more than two sessions, before you even get to grips with the main issues. I guarantee it probably took years to get you into an issue, we must be patient as we struggle to get out, bearing in mind the opposition against us to do that.

Most of the principles encapsulated within this short booklet will take consistent practice before they become a part of your everyday life. Up to this point a language of the soul has been developed within you, it is a language you internalised and were successful in not allowing it to surface, but it has become a way you 'talk to yourself.'

To develop and speak a new language is going to require you to practice it, this will involve surrounding yourself with those who also speak the same language, immerse yourself in it, change the environment you have become accustomed to.

Sexual sin requires an internal language of lust. You have been taught to respond when stimulated with indulgence, through the years you have trained yourself to indulge your lust and as a result this language becomes internalised. I know of those who had their favourite movies or images they would use for masturbating, websites they would visit, chat rooms they would haunt, texting partners, the communication channels are so numerous. To change the language will mean closing down all these avenues that lust will take you down. Developing a new language means first of all confronting REPETITIVELY, eventually you will become fluent.

Tools to help:

Within the context of mind attack, it is simply a time to refocus; breathe; count. It is time to give yourself, in which to cool down physically and mentally, leaving you an extra moment in which to make the right choice and introduce your own trusted 'counter-measures.'[30]

Reality Check! Another means of refocussing, getting your mind out of fantasy and back into the realm of reality. Spend a moment verbally reaffirming your true identity, who you are, what your real priorities are, the names of your partner, children, even grandchildren,

---

[30] 1 Peter 1:13, Matthew 6:22.

your position within your church, your pastors. Then remind yourself what you stand to lose if your subsequent actions lead you to acting out. It may be a time to even call an accountability partner.

This can act like a mental and verbal cold shower and snap you back from the edge of imaginations, remembering that God has given us what we need, including the power, to deal with anything that opposes God.[31] It is a good exercise, as it is much more difficult to entertain a sexual fantasy whilst verbalising these things.

One of the things we do when tempted is to build a secret room in our minds (a stronghold), we block out the real world within which we normally exist. Another speaking out exercise that is effective is to recount what is likely to occur if your private world becomes public. What will it do to those around you? What will it do to you? Do you think you would even survive? Will your faith survive? Do you know of others who have fallen away never to return to either their faith or their families? There is real power in speaking out that which is true and noble, affirming those things.[32]

Thinking is all important to our being successful in confronting the attacks when they come. Asking questions concerning ourselves is also good. Is this a trigger, a mood, maybe a wound or unresolved issue? Has this temptation come as a result of something

---

[31] 2 Corinthians 10:3-5.
[32] Philippians 4:8.

beyond my control like a pop-up or an advertising board, or is it a result of me being foolish, playing/flirting with something I know is wrong? Not to condemn ourselves, but to deal with self-deception.

Those questions should determine our immediate response. If it is a wound that is once again causing pain, perhaps it has been unattended for some time, or even ignored. Self-care is an imperative for us all. There is a useful acronym that can easily be remembered. HALT (Hungry, Angry, Lonely, Tired).

There is a difference between appetite and hunger, especially within the context of sexual purity. Appetite can be a lie that your body tells you which is more about what you want and not necessarily about what you need. Indulgence in sexual sin can train you to become more aware of gratification than real satisfaction. In other words, we need to learn how to deal with frustration and see the impact short and long term of our subsequent decisions. The longer we seek to satisfy our appetite, the less able we are to distinguish it from hunger. Hunger is about what you really need, and hunger does not lie.

If you develop a lifestyle that is more focussed on satisfying appetites, you learn to choose short term pleasure that may bring long-term discomfort – not a good investment. In refusing to pander to the appetite, may involve some short-term discomfort, but will definitely bring long-term peace. Sexual acting out, more often than not, involves seeking an intense or 'hyper-stimulating' experience; however, it will not bring complete satisfaction, as it does not involve real intimacy.

A person can easily become addicted to intensity and mistake it for intimacy, but the intensity will lead to only seeking deeper intensity, which may eventually lead to all kinds of perversions. Intimacy leads to knowing and being known (which is a creational mandate). Sexual acting out gives the illusion by creating intensity, but denies the benefits of really knowing and being known. An affair may well begin in an intensity that at times blows the persons mind, however, pay day comes sooner or later and before long, they feel trapped, empty and very dissatisfied. More often than not the affair leaves you right where you started, only this time the next intense experience will need to be even more pleasurable. Just like drugs. The road to nowhere.

Chapter Five - Travailing – lasting the course, pushing through to victory

Another motivational point to make at this juncture of the course, is that the longer you are able to maintain your sexual purity, engaging in your new disciplines, experiencing a new mindset, the more motivated you will be to protect them. However, it is vital we do not begin to develop either a Pharasaical attitude, or the mis-belief that it is all down to our own abilities. We will always need God's grace and mercy, every Christian knows that, *"God in His Grace gives us what we do not deserve, God in His mercy does not give us what we do deserve."* His forgiveness love and presence in our lives, keep us and constantly restores us to Himself.

The apostle Paul is a great example to us, after his amazing statement in the bible,[33] Paul had his battles, understanding that every time you resist temptation you are resisting evil, you may not win every battle, but you can still win the war. We aim not only to finish this race, but to finish well, maintaining a lifestyle commensurate with our stated beliefs.

To travail simply means to labour or toil, which is why the term is more often used in connection with a woman's travailing in pregnancy.

---

[33] 2 Timothy 4:7.

To bring anything that is of Christ to birth in our lives will involve a travailing, a toiling, an enduring quality that is not 'caught' but is developed through discipline and courage. Anything of Christ in your life will be opposed.[34] Whenever something of Christ is birthed from within you, it is opposed and stolen, or potentially swallowed up.

It is entirely possible that you experience the discouragement of relapse, which is a breaking of your own rules or definition of what it is to be sexually pure. It is therefore important that you understand what a break in your determination to be sexually pure is.

An example definition might be:

- Abstinence from pornography.
- Avoiding illegitimate forms of sexual stimulation.
- Sexual acting out of any kind that involves another person, including masturbation that depends largely upon fantasy or looking at pornographic images.
- Committing to a form of confession that helps develop a lifestyle of 'dragging out' of darkness, to bring into light hidden threats to purity.
- Telling my accountability partner when I am struggling – Adam's response was to hide, refuse to hide any longer.
- Seeking to understand what went wrong when, how, why, do I need a new strategy?

---

[34] Revelation 12 – the whole chapter.

Relapse does not have to be the end; a valley was never meant to become a graveyard. There are some obvious precursors to relapse that are worth making a note of:

1. Avoid triumphalism – When anyone goes into recovery they find after a few weeks that things have greatly improved in their life. They mistakenly take the attitude that they are fixed and no longer see the need of maintaining new disciplines, or become lazy or even arrogant. It's a little like someone on medication, 'the pills are working now so I can stop taking them.' Understand that not all needs are 'felt.'
2. Unwillingness – to be honest about weaknesses therefore hiding them rather than confessing them out of either pride or fear of disappointing those around us. The temptation here is to present ourselves as something more than we are when we think we are improving.[35]
3. Unwillingness – to address deeper emotional issues that may be part of the problem. When we get involved in any kind of sexual sin, it is usually because there are legitimate needs that we are seeking to meet in illegitimate ways.

We need to know what the legitimate needs are and learn to meet them in legitimate ways. When you are in recovery, it is because of decisions that YOU have made, but it is vital that we discover any emotional issues or past trauma's that have contributed to the decisions being made. This is NOT to use them as excuses or

---

[35] "Imperfect authenticity is better than inauthentic perfection."

justifying behaviour, but change is not change until it involves change.

At the very start of this course, we noted God's intention that the sons of God are revealed. This is God's intention for every person, that they are ultimately revealed as his child, it is the reason we were born again, God initiated, sustains and completes this work as we learn to cooperate with Him.[36]

You are part of a 'band of brother' (or sisters), who have all found the need for maintenance or recovery, even Jesus declared that it is those who know their need for a doctor that really need Him. Most people have not had the opportunity to engage in a recovery group or accountability group, therefore they have struggled perhaps for a long time to deal with this alone, most if not all find that is impossible.

Robert Bly said, *"Where a man's greatest wound is, there too is his genius."*

Corrie Ten Boom said, *"They'll believe us because we've been there."*

I honestly believe that the battle for sexual purity is one of, if not the biggest and potentially most damaging areas of sin facing the Church today. Men, women and young people are being isolated from all sources of help and we are living in a culture that is in crisis. You can still make

---

[36] Romans8:19.

a difference in this environment. By being a part of the Waythrough Solutions Trust partnership we are bringing this whole area into the light. Everyone knows it is there, but we are reluctant to deal with it, mainly because it will mean vulnerability, humility, transparency, no more mask wearing. During the earliest days of Methodism, they had what they called 'holiness groups,' where men and women learned to be real.

Martin Luthor King Jr said, *"The conscience of the state is being revived which is the only hope for the state."*

The Church can and will become the attractive alternative because many men and women are already becoming sickened by their addictions and are desperate for sources of help. So, what's the problem, why don't people reach out? Fear!

Beginning in this arena of ministry has meant huge steps of faith and sacrifice needing to be made. We have sought out new modalities that have often been misunderstood, we have known rejection, irrelevance, loss of perceived status, loss of income, misunderstandings, however – we have become a 'safe place.'

People have sought us out, pastors, believers across the denominations, unbelievers, people who believed their lives were spiralling out of control. Not only in the sexual arena. People who have suffered at the hands of those within a religious system that has lost its heart. The Church must be ready to deal compassionately, non-judgementally with an area of sin that will remain hidden, keeping the church powerless because many of its members have been emasculated through these soulish attacks, in an area of their lives that are so vulnerable.

Today may be your day to deal with your recovery, tomorrow it will be time to pass on what you have and still are learning to someone who is hungry for help. "They will believe you, because you have been there."

Conclusions

*T*urn around (repent), after realising that sexual sin was corrupting my life, meant God had to intervene with a crisis of truth. I have and still am identifying: -

*R*ules, through which I am beginning to establish new structures and disciplines in my life, aimed at helping my recovery process and maintenance of my sexual purity.

*U*nderstanding has helped me to gain insight and clarity, giving me tools to be a good steward of my mind and body, knowing what the triggers are that I need to avoid, my wounds, my moods, all of which can contribute to the cycles of temptation we all experience.

*S*trategy is helping me to avoid moving from stimulation into indulgence and how to appreciate the differences between intimacy and intensity.

*T*ravailing is helping me to avoid relapsing, to know that relapse is NOT inevitable, that I can move on from here into greater depths of recovery, perhaps even getting to the place where I am able to help others into their rightful place as children of God.[37]

---

[37] Psalm 138:8.

TRUST Partnerships

This booklet has been produced with a view to using it as a resource for hosting small groups of men and women who are seeking to establish or maintain their sobriety.

For any help or advice David can be contacted via email at pastordavidcrabb@gmail.com

Printed in Poland
by Amazon Fulfillment
Poland Sp. z o.o., Wrocław

60695973R00040